Up on Deck

Written by Catherine Baker
Illustrated by Estelle Corke

Collins

The sun is hot.

I am up on deck.

I am not hot.

4

The sun hat is red.

A pup has a run...

in the hot sun.

A rat hops on rocks.

Up, up it hops.

A duck sits and pecks.

It pecks the mud.

A tap and a peck.

Up pops a duck!

/r/

14

15

 After reading

Letters and Sounds: Phase 2

Word count: 54

Focus phonemes: /o/ ck /e/ /u/ /r/ /h/

Common exception words: the, is, I, has

Curriculum links: Understanding the World: The World

Early learning goals: Listening and attention: listen to stories, accurately anticipating key events and respond to what is heard with relevant comments, questions or actions; Understanding: answer 'how' and 'why' questions about experiences and in response to stories or events; Reading: children use phonic knowledge to decode regular words and read them aloud accurately

Developing fluency

- Go back and read the story to your child, using lots of expression.
- Make sure that your child follows as you read.
- Pause so that they can join in and read with you.
- Say the whole chant together. You can make up some actions to go with the words.

Phonic practice

- The words below all have the /ck/ phoneme (letter sound) in them.

d/e/ck	deck	p/e/ck/s	pecks
d/u/ck	duck	l/u/ck	luck

- Say the sounds, then ask your child to repeat the sounds and say the word.
- If your child cannot work out what the word is, say the sounds, and then say the word. Tell your child to repeat after you.
- Now look at the 'I spy sounds' on pages 14 and 15 together. Which words can your child find in the picture with the 'r' sound in them? (e.g. *robin, red, rocket, robot, rat, reeds, riders, rocks*). How about the letter 'h'? (e.g. *helicopter, hippo, horses, hat, hamper*).